Highland Costume

John Telfer Dunbar

JOHN TELFER DUNBAR is President of the Saint Andrew Society of Scotland, President of The Costume Society of Scotland and a Fellow of the Society of Antiquaries of Scotland. He is a former Honorary Curator of the Scottish United Services Museum.

For over thirty years he has broadcast and lectured on Scottish costume and uniforms, and his writings have been translated into French, German and Spanish.

The author's collection of early Scottish costume, tartans, manuscripts and pictures is world famous. Part of it was gifted to the City of Edinburgh, where it is on permanent exhibition in the Tolbooth.

Cover illustration: from Jas Logan's *Scottish Gael*, 1831

HIGHLAND COSTUME

John Telfer Dunbar

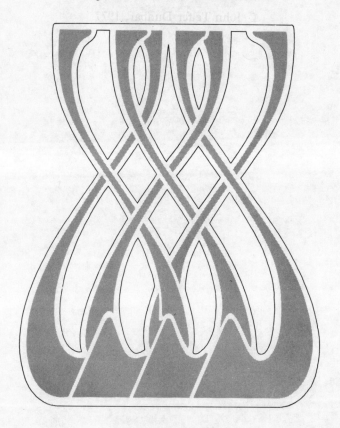

**JAMES THIN
THE MERCAT PRESS, EDINBURGH**

First published in 1977.
Reprinted by James Thin,
53-59 South Bridge,
Edinburgh, in 1983

ISBN 0 901824 74 7

Printed by William Blackwood & Sons Ltd,
162 Leith Walk,
Edinburgh EH6 5DX

To my wife
Elizabeth

Contents

The Historical Background   1

Tartan   6

Before the Kilt   17

The Kilt   33

Prince Charles Edward Stuart   46

Highland Ladies   54

Reading List   61

Illustrations

(Illustrations marked thus* are in the author's collection)

Carding and spinning yarn in the Highlands* 9

Highland lassies waulking tartan, 1770* 13

French version of 'Wild Scots', 1562* 22

Engravings by Van der Gucht, showing the belted
 plaid, 1743* 26

Highland Chief by J. Michael Wright, *c.* 1660
(Scottish National Portrait Gallery) 27

Major Fraser of Castle Leathers, 1670-1750
(Inverness District Council) 29

Sir John Sinclair by Sir Henry Raeburn, 1794
(National Gallery of Scotland) 31

The Macdonald Boys, *c.* 1750
(The Rt Hon. Lord Macdonald) 37

Les Écossais à Paris, ou la curiosité des femmes,
 Paris, 1815* 39

King George IV and Sir William Curtis, 1822* 43

The Duke of Leeds. Engraving after painting by
 Hans Hysing, 1726* 49

Prince Charles Edward Stuart. Engraving by
 Richard Cooper, 1745* 50

Helen Murray of Ochtertyre, *c.* 1745
(Anthony Murray, Esq.) 59

The Historical Background

AMONG the national costumes of the world, that of the Scot is unique. It combines two very significant aspects, namely the remembrance of great episodes in the history of the country and the pride of its wearer in his or her family or name. No other national costume has this significant and personal depth of meaning and, perhaps because of this, very few other civilian costumes can arouse the emotions which our kilts and tartans have done for centuries.

It is therefore rather important that before we examine the form and evolution of the dress itself, we consider the historical background against which it evolved.

The emergence of Scottish Highland dress as a recognisable entity took place several centuries ago in that happy hunting ground for antiquarians known as the 'Mists of Antiquity'. Any attempt to fix its obscure origins precisely is undoubtedly foolish; nevertheless many students of the subject have attempted to do so. Their resulting arguments have usually generated more heat than light.

These origins were governed to some extent by Gaelic and Irish ethnic influences, but they were also governed, to a larger extent, by environmental conditions. The whims of fashion played no significant part in these early origins as the dress was worn by people distant from the world of modes and manners. Indeed, what is now worn and recognised universally as our national costume, originated in the mid-seventeenth century as the dress of a small impoverished section of the Scottish nation living in a remote and inhospitable part of the country. However, while they struggled for centuries against economic poverty, this minority group were to gain a wealth of romantic tradition and stirring history perpetuated in song and story and, most of all, in costume.

The historical episodes which we might describe as the

opening chapters of our story were the Jacobite Risings of the first half of the eighteenth century, when the House of Stewart attempted to overthrow the reigning House of Hanover.

In their attempt to overthrow the Government, both the 'Old Pretender' and the 'Young Pretender' sought and won the support of Highland chiefs. It followed, then, that when the Jacobites were defeated at the Battle of Culloden in 1746, their Highland costume became a symbol of rebellion which sprang into the light of history. The victors applied the age-old methods of stamping out the national pride of their victims, and these included the banning of their costume which was regarded as a dangerous symbol which might in time rekindle the old fires.

It came about this way. After a proposed series of Disarming Acts, came the Act of 1746 (Geo, II c 39) in which it was decreed:

> 'That from and after the First Day of August, One thousand seven hundred and forty-seven, no Man or Boy, within that part of Great Britain called Scotland, other than such as shall be employed as Officers and Soldiers in His Majesty's Forces, shall, on any pretence whatsoever, wear or put on the Clothes commonly called Highland Clothes (that is to say) the Plaid, Philebeg, or little Kilt, Trowse, Shoulder Belts, or any Part whatsoever of what peculiarly belongs to the Highland Garb; and that no Tartan, or party-coloured Plaid or Stuff shall be used for Great Coats, or for Upper Coats. . . .'

The penalty for a first offence was six months' imprisonment, and for a second offence, transportation to the Plantations for the space of seven years.

The Act was applied in a most unsatisfactory way, even to some of the clansmen who had remained loyal to the Government. Its effect was described by a certain Captain Burt in his *Letters from a Gentleman in the North of Scotland*, published in 1754. He considered that because Highland dress served as both costume and sleeping-bag, and because its colours provided ideal camouflage in both cases, it was therefore ideal for evil intentions and 'instant rebellion'. On the other hand, it allowed the wearer to 'skip over the rocks and bogs' when travelling upon his lawful purposes. Burt's final objection to the Act was that whereas the Highlander could purchase his dress for a few shillings, a Lowland suit would be beyond his means.

Lord President Forbes attempted to persuade the Government to adopt a more humane policy, but without success. They reacted by proposing a barbarous oath to be taken by suspects, who had to swear that they would never use any 'tartan, plaid, or any part of the Highland garb'. The oath concluded:

> 'If I do so, may I be cursed in my undertakings, family, and property—may I never see my wife and children, father, mother, and relations—may I be killed in battle as a coward, and lie without Christian burial, in a strange land far from the graves of my forefathers and kindred;—may all this come across me if I break my oath.'

It was not until 1782 that this proscription was repealed by a Bill introduced by the Duke of Montrose. But now the revival of the Highland dress and tartans was to be affected by European history. The revolutionary drums were beating in France, and the second chapter of our history of Scottish costume begins.

In 1766 William Pitt declared before Parliament that he sought military merit wherever he could find it, and find it he did—'in the mountains of the North'. During the seventy-five years before the Battle of Waterloo, over a hundred battalions of the line, militia, fencibles and volunteers were raised in the Highlands. During that time the Highland military uniform won renown far from its native heath, and after the final defeat of Napoleon it was once more worn with pride by civilians in and out of the Highlands. Moreover, as we shall see later, it now took on a military style which has remained till today.

The next historical event which had an immense effect on

3

the history of Highland dress was short in duration but extremely wide in influence. It might be said, somewhat ungraciously, that the same dimensions applied to the person who played the principal part in the event—His Majesty King George the Fourth.

In 1822 he agreed to pay a State Visit to Scotland, the arrangements for which were placed in the hands of Sir Walter Scott and David Stewart of Garth. Despite a few protests, the nation plunged into a tartan frenzy, especially once the news was spread that the king and Sir William Curtis, Lord Mayor of London, were both to appear in Highland dress (see the illustration on page 43).

The romantic nature of the Scots was poised for just such an event. Scott had created a lasting impression that the Highlands and the Highlanders were 'picturesque'. Lady Nairn's songs were the perfect accompaniment to a wave of Jacobite sentimentality. The 'Celtic Club' were dedicated to promoting the revival of Highland costume. Sir Walter's son-in-law, John Gibson Lockhart, described the result as a Celtic hallucination, an expression which could not be applied to the accounts of the tartan manufacturers. It has been estimated that the number of clan tartans increased tenfold within three weeks.

The Marchioness of Tullibardine wrote that many of the Highland chiefs and nobles were 'drilling their tenants to appear as Highland clansmen of patriarchal times' and, in fact, some of them almost bankrupted their estates in order to outshine their fellows in splendour. But it was not only the Highlanders who took to the 'Garb of Old Gaul', Lowlanders flocked to their tailors with demands for immediate delivery of Highland costumes. The fact that these costumes were largely designed for the levee, the ballroom and the assembly, meant that the emphasis was on the spectacular—far removed from the clothes worn by the Highlanders in their native hills. The dress in its new form was now the Scottish National Dress.

The enthusiasm which began in 1822 never waned. The Victorians found the dress highly respectable, especially

4

when Prince Albert took to it, and the rage for tartan scarfs and skirts, worn by the Queen herself, quickly spread throughout Europe. Who had not heard of John Brown?

Much older than the kilt, however, was the material of which it was made. The 'clan' tartans as we know them today cannot claim an origin earlier than the mid-eighteenth century, and few of them were born much before the visit of George the Fourth. Nevertheless 'tartan' has been worn for centuries longer than the kilt, and it is logical therefore that we consider the cloth before we consider the clothes.

Tartan

ONLY a very small percentage of the inhabitants of Scotland
are regular wearers of tartan today. However, its use and
misuse can arouse strong emotions—particularly among
those living outside the Highlands. I doubt if any other
national costume has the same emotive power, and several
writers have gone to great lengths to ascribe the greatest
possible antiquity to Scottish clan tartans. Indeed, one Victorian writer had the splendid notion—with ack-
nowledgements to Julius Caesar—that they originated with
early races painting 'coloured stripes on their knees and
lower limbs, so denoting the families or septs to which they
belonged'.

It is, in fact, very difficult to say at what stage early
fabrics became definable as 'Tartans'. A piece of Roman
cloth discovered in Scotland has been described as
'tartan', and so have fabrics from Corsica, Burma, Norway
and Russia. The fact is that any fabric, the pattern of the
warp and weft of which being similar, will look like a
tartan.

The very word itself had different meanings at different
times and at different places. In 1538 a word appeared which
is often quoted as the first reference to tartan in Scotland. In
that year the Lord High Treasurer's Accounts describe a
Highland dress which was made for King James the Fifth
and which consisted of 'ane schort Heland Coit' made of
varicoloured velvet, and trews which required three ells of
'Heland tertane to be hoiss'. His long shirts, 'Heland Sarkis',
were made of 'Holland claith'. Unfortunately several
modern writers have misquoted the original spelling of the
word 'tertane' and given it as 'tartan'.

Also frequently misquoted is the French word *tiretaine*,
associated with the Spanish word *tiritana*, both of which refer
to a type of cloth regardless of its design. And, for good

6

measure, there is a rare word 'tuartan' which occurs in certain Irish manuscripts.

In fact the Highlanders never used such a word in speaking their native Gaelic. The word they used to describe tartan was *breacan*, which is defined by the renowned authority Campbell of Islay as meaning 'spotted like a trout, banded like a zebra, or striped cross-wise'.

It is only when we come to the definition of 'clan' tartans that we are on slightly more solid ground. But it is only as solid as a Highland bog.

The early specimens of tartan which we know to have been made and worn in the Highlands, and which belong to the early eighteenth century, are very rare. Campbell of Islay and Alexander Carmichael—author of *Carmina Gadelica*—were the earliest collectors to realise the importance of these lovely specimens of Highland artistry and skill. Many of them are now in my collection and are described and illustrated in my *History of Highland Dress*.

They are, of course, quite unlike the later 'clan' tartans both in complexity and design. But it is perhaps the colouring of these rare textiles which first attracts the eye.

There is considerable obscurity surrounding the subject of Highland dyes, and this may be partly due to the fact that they were never produced in large enough quantities to be used for commercial purposes. They were created in the glens and seldom passed out of them. Many of the old recipes were probably forgotten during the period of almost a generation when the tartan was proscribed after 1746. Then, when Highland dress began to be worn once more, foreign dyestuffs were available and cloth was being produced on a factory basis. The death-knell of organic dyeing sounded in the mid-nineteenth century when chemical dyestuffs swept the market.

During the eighteenth century the variations in the colours produced by means of organic dyes were immense. Experiments which I carried out over a period of years demonstrated that the same dye recipe gave a considerable range of colours according to climate and habitat. The mineral content of the water, the maturity of the flora involved, and the widely varying temperatures and times, all contributed to the wide range of shades and colours which resulted when eighteenth-century methods and equipment were used. To produce a standard set of colours in any quantity under such conditions was not possible.

Moreover, the hard wool of the Highland sheep added to the difficulty of producing constant colours, and sometimes the wool had to be soaked for weeks to get the dye to hold. In some cases the dyeing was done by the Highlanders before the wool was spun, but more often it was the yarn that was dyed. The scarcity of large iron pots which could be spared for weeks, and the labour involved in keeping up a stock of fuel were further reasons why the production of coloured yarn was difficult. It is obvious that clothing made from natural, undyed wool and from yarn of a single easily produced colour must have been widely used by the impoverished Highlanders.

Lichens provided yellow dyes and many shades of brown, which was a colour also produced from the bark of trees. The water-lily provided black and grey after a tedious process, but it often faded into green. Crimson and purple came from *corcur*, the basic ingredient of which was human urine. Red could be obtained from Ladies Bedstraw, and a beautiful blue-grey from sliced-up roots of the Yellow Iris.

Once the wool was dyed it was combed out in order to straighten the fibres and produce a more uniform density. At a later date this was done with a pair of carders—flat boards with wire teeth.

Spinning the wool into yarn was originally done with the distaff and spindle or, as they were sometimes called in Scotland, the rock and reel. Having tied the wool to the distaff this was then tucked under the left arm or sometimes into the belt. Some twisted fibres were then teased from the wool and fastened to a notch on the end of the spindle. The latter was given a twirl, and as it turned it twisted the fibres into yarn. When a convenient length had been spun, the yarn was wound round the spindle and the process repeated. This

8

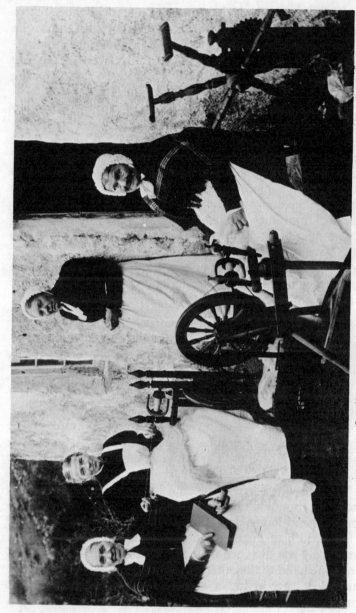

Carding and spinning yarn in the Highlands

kind of spinning could be done while tending the stock or even while carrying sea-weed from the shore to fertilise the lazy-beds. This was made possible by the fact that the baskets were often carried by head-bands. Even in the late nineteenth century this method was in use—spindles were made from a potato with a stick through the centre.

The 'Muckle Wheel' which followed the distaff and spindle produced the yarn much faster, but it was a static process. The wheel was rotated with one hand while the other held the wool, paying it out as the yarn was spun. It was then wound back on to the spindle. This type of spinning-wheel was gradually replaced during the eighteenth century by the 'little' or 'Saxony' wheel which was operated by a treadle. The twisting and winding of the yarn was now achieved in one operation. Wheels of this type are still in use (see page 9).

As part of the attempt to pacify the Highlands and encourage cottage industry after Culloden, spinning schools were started in many districts. A factor in Crieff gave his opinion:

'There are crowds of little Girls here that Stroll about the streets playing at hand Ball and other such Employments and Diversions who might be usefully employed in Spinning.'

In fact it was said that the Rising of 1745 had introduced 'little wheels and red soldiers'.

After spinning, the yarn was wound on to a simple frame or reel known by several names according to district—such as the 'Little Horse' or 'The Knives' (seen on the right of the photograph).

Weaving was carried out on a large upright loom which occupied about half of the weaver's cottage. There were also smaller hand-looms and garter looms.

The width of material woven on the old hand-loom was limited by the distance which the shuttle could be thrown from one hand to the other. In general this was a little under three feet, producing a slightly narrower material after shrinkage. The belted plaid required a double width sewn together down the centre.

Although there is plenty of information about weaving and weavers in the Lowlands, little is known about their Highland cousins. Weavers were said to be devious folk, and a popular expression was 'crooked as a weaver'. It might be charitable to think of this as referring to his physical appearance, resulting from crouching over the loom.

Once the cloth was woven, the next process was one which perpetuated a great deal of Highland song and story. This was the 'waulking' or fulling of the cloth. After being soaked in an alkaline solution, the cloth was thoroughly beaten and worked by hand to thicken it and close up the threads. This was done on a long board originally made of wattle and latterly of ridged wood. Having placed the cloth on the board a group of about ten women sat down on either side and began the process of tossing and pummelling the cloth with their hands and feet (see page 13). It was then that the folk-tales and songs began. Many of these referred to old tales and traditions; others were based on the latest news or scandal. Alexander Carmichael published many of the songs in his magnificent *Carmina Gadelica*.

When the whole process of making the cloth was over, it was carefully stretched and rolled up. In some cases it was then blessed and consecrated. If the material was intended for more than one person, all those who were to receive a piece of the cloth might be mentioned in the blessing. Alexander Carmichael makes a reference to this when he quotes the following verse of a waulking chant:

'This is not the cloth for priest or cleric,
But it is cloth for my own little Donald of love,
For my companion beloved, for John of joy,
And for Muriel of loveliest hue.'

It may be that this emotional regard for Highland costume contributed towards the feelings which have survived to this day. Certainly when, at a later date, the pattern or sett of a tartan was used to identify the personal name or affiliation of the wearer, the kilt became an emotive object. The historical events with which tartan began to be associated added to this feeling, and even in the unromantic times in which we live today, it is a hard-hearted individual who cannot feel some emotion at the sight and sound of the pipes and drums on parade, or the lone piper playing on the battlements of Edinburgh Castle during the Tattoo.

If we examine the pictorial and documentary evidence of the patterns of tartan worn before Culloden we cannot find evidence which supports a theory of organised or 'clan' tartans. Until fairly recent times, however, there have been many attempts to do so. In seeking to ascribe great antiquity to modern clan tartans, the most obscure of the early references have been quoted. But these references, by nature of their very obscurity, can be used in counter-argument.

Like the Highland dress itself, no precise original dates can be given to the personal clan tartan idea. It is in the field of military history that we are most likely to find the early implications and origins of the modern clan tartan. In 1725, very shortly after the widespread emergence of military uniform in general, the Highland Independent Companies were raised and dressed in the belted plaid. Developing into the Black Watch, they were issued with a uniform tartan which, incidentally, was to become the basis of many other military and civilian tartans. During the Jacobite Rising the only means of telling Jacobite from Hanoverian by his dress was to examine the colour of his cockade. If it was white he was a Jacobite, but the colour of his tartan, if he wore any, gave no indication as to his allegiance. Again it must be remembered that during the time of the Proscription only the Highland regiments were allowed to wear the tartan. They wore tartans which were uniform and from which one could tell the identity of the regiment.

If we examine a contemporary painting of the Battle of Culloden painted by an artist renowned for his accuracy, we find evidence of the true nature of tartan designs in 1746. The picture, now in the Royal Collection, was painted for the Duke of Cumberland by David Morier. His painting of Barrell's Regiment being attacked by the Jacobite forces

Highland lassies waulking tartan, 1770

13

shows at least twenty-three tartans being worn by eight Highlanders, and not a single pattern can be identified as that of any modern clan tartan. (A full description of these tartans is contained in *History of Highland Dress*.)

The best and earliest evidence of the growth of clan tartans is contained in the records of the firm of William Wilson and Sons Ltd which started to manufacture tartans at Bannockburn during the third quarter of the eighteenth century. By 1794, they were supplying the 42nd Regiment with Officers Plaid tartan and Officers Kilt tartan. Very soon they had virtually achieved a monopoly in the supply of civilian tartans and tartans for use as furnishings. They invented many 'fancy' tartans and designed many clan and district patterns. They even exported to the Americas in the early 1800s when tartans were used to clothe slaves.

It is interesting to notice the growth of patterns, or setts, as time passed. In the 1790s, Wilson's list numbered about forty patterns. These included many identified by number only, and others described as 'Blanket Tartan, Red and White Tartan, Black and Red Tartan, Green Ground Plaids', etc. By 1800, the number had doubled with a considerable increase in the patterns known by number only, and the addition of such setts as 'Aberdeen Sett, Athol pattern, Crief [*sic*] Sett, Perth Sett, Waggrall, Ritch, Lasting, Glasgow, Birral, Gallowater, Caledonian', etc. Wilson's were inventing new tartans all the time, partly due to the competition from firms of tartan manufacturers in Norwich. The Bannockburn tartans were made in a variety of materials ranging from the cheap coarse quality to the superfine wool material, sometimes having a silk line added to 'liven' it up.

Tartans were also given the names of the towns in which they were popular and had the greatest sales. At a later date they were even given the names of the firm's travellers. By 1810 Wilson's tartans were so widely known that a forger who escaped from the jail at Inverness was described as wearing 'a light green tartan coat of the Bannockburn manufacture'.

By the time of King George the Fourth's visit in 1822,

there were scores of patterns known by numbers, and the firm's correspondence contains many references to 'new' and 'latest' patterns. But whereas the number of patterns having fancy names or numbers increased rapidly, those having 'clan' names did not. In the early nineteenth century the total was still under fifty, today it is well over one thousand. The source of many of today's setts is obscure and frequently the subject of hot debate. For the purpose of status, there is often a desire to claim an antiquity for a tartan, but why an ancient pattern is superior to a more recent one is not quite clear.

From what has been stated earlier, it is obvious that the materials and means available to the eighteenth-century Highlander did not allow him to manufacture any considerable quantity of tartan of uniform pattern. Modern factory methods, however, enable us to do so today, and when we refer to modern clan tartans we talk of 'Correct' or even 'Official' setts. We also talk of 'Correct' colours, and even of 'Authentic' colours. To produce such uniformity would not have been possible with organic dyes, but owing to the use of modern chemical dyes, it is now simple. In fact some very lovely colours can be reproduced, and these are often described as 'Ancient' tartans although the actual pattern may not be ancient.

In its modern context, it is obviously desirable to reach some agreement over what is, or is not, the accepted pattern or sett to be worn. Methods of recording and describing the setts have now evolved and can be used easily.

The design of a clan tartan might appear to be complicated, but it is in fact quite simple. The weave is known as twill—that is to say, it goes 'over two and under two'. The warp and the weft are identical in the width of their bands or lines, and in their colour sequence. Where two of the same colour cross they produce a pure colour, but where two different colours cross they produce a tint by their mixture. There is no such thing as a tartan of the 'correct' size; it is the proportions which must be correct. This means that a system can be devised whereby the correct 'sett' of a tartan can be recorded, and from this it can be reproduced in any size.

15

These setts have been recorded on *The Official Tartan Map* and in other publications.

So from the early beginnings when tartans were made from local materials in quantities governed by their availability, they have evolved to the 'clan' patterns produced in vast quantities in many countries today. From the beautiful hand-woven cloth worn by a minority of the Highlanders and chosen according to fancy, the modern tartan has become not only the emblem of Scotland but also an expression of individual recognition.

As the history of tartan unwound in the manner described, so the way in which it was worn went through many stages. Because the evidence is scarce, obscure and often contradictory, it is not easy to simplify. Perhaps this is what gives it a fascination and provides students with a splendid battleground for their arguments.

Before the Kilt

THE ancient dress of the Scottish and Irish Gael consisted of a shirt or smock known as the *léine* (Gaelic), and a semicircular mantle known as the *brat* (Gaelic). This dress was worn by men and women alike, but in a longer form by the women. In addition, there was another item of dress which has survived to the present day, namely the 'trews'. It may well be that the latter was the dress of pre-Gaelic people, and it was the conquering Gaels who wore the loose garments. Again it might well be that the brat-and-léine costume was worn by the chiefs and warriors, and the jacket-and-trews by the humbler folk.

It is almost entirely to Ireland that we must look for evidence of the early forms of Gaelic dress. The trews, worn both long to the ankle and short to the knee, were in use as early as the eighth century and are illustrated in the magnificent Book of Kells, generally admitted to date from the middle of the eighth century. The ancestry of the brat-and-léine can almost certainly be traced to pre-Christian times.

Both costumes continued in use, in varying forms, up to the end of the sixteenth century. At that time the *brat* was made of strong woollen cloth of any colour, and it often had a thick shaggy pile on the outside to give additional warmth. The *léine* was generally made of saffron-yellow linen and known in English as a 'Saffron Shirt'. It was worn in long and short styles, and had sleeves and a wide pleated skirt for mobility. The fact that this skirt was mistaken by some writers for a separate 'kilt' has caused confusion in the past.

A form of the brat-and-léine costume is described in the Saga of Magnus Berfaet, dated A.D. 1093. When he returned from one of his expeditions he acquired his name by adopting the manner of dress in use in western lands and going about bare-legged, 'having short kyrtles and upper garments'.

17

In a Latin history of the First Crusade written about 1110, a Picard describes the Scottish soldiers '. . . bare-legged with their shaggy cloaks, a scrip hanging *ex humeris*, coming from their marshy homeland'. It is tempting to describe the 'scrip' as an early sporran and, in fact, the same author describes devils 'wearing their scrips in the manner of the Scots, hanging forward from their haunches, as they are wont'.

In 1521, a Scot, John Major, wrote a *History of Greater Britain* in Latin. He describes the dress of the Highlanders in detail thus:

> 'From the middle of the thigh to the foot they have no covering for the leg, clothing themselves with a mantle instead of an upper garment and a shirt dyed with saffron. . . . In time of war they cover their whole body with a shirt of mail or iron rings, and fight in that. The common people of the Highland Scots rush into battle having their body clothed with a linen garment manifoldly sewed and painted or daubed with pitch, with a covering of deerskin.'

Obviously bare legs were a distinguishing feature of the appearance of the early Highlanders, and accepted as such not only by visitors but also by the natives themselves. A certain John Elder wrote to King Henry the Eighth on the subject of a proposed union between Scotland and England. In his letter he describes at great length the merits of Highland dress:

> 'Moreover . . . we of all people can tolleratt, suffir, and always best with cold, for boithe somer and wyntir, (excepte whene the froest is mooste vehement) goynge alwaise bair leggide and bair footide, our delite and pleasure is not only in huntynge . . . but also in rynninge, leaping, swymynge, shootynge, and thrawinge of dartis; therfor, in so moche as we use and delite so to go alwais, the tendir delicatt gentillmen of Scotland call us Red-shanckes.'

I think this is one of the most delightful descriptions of sixteenth-century life in the Highlands.

18

The title Redshanks stuck, and in the 1570s, Lindsay of Pitscottie referred to 'the Reidschankis, or wyld Scottis . . . cloathed with ane mantle, with ane schirt saffroned after the Irisch maner, going bair legged to the knie'.

The Latin account of the Highlanders given by the Bishop of Ross in 1578 is one of the most important to survive from an eye-witness. He points out that their costume was designed for use and not for ornament. Both nobles and common people wore mantles, but those of the nobility were more colourful. Being long and flowing, they served as dress by day and blanket by night. The rest of their garments consisted of a short woollen jacket with open sleeves, and a covering for the thighs of the simplest kind, 'more for decency than for show or defence against cold'. The Bishop also mentions large linen shirts with numerous folds and wide sleeves, sewn up with red and green silk thread. Some were coloured with saffron, and others were smeared with grease to preserve them during their constant warlike exercises.

An important element of the warlike activities of a mountain people is the need for concealment, and it is at this time that we come upon a reference to the need for camouflage in dress. In 1581, George Buchanan, a Stirlingshire historian, published a full description of the Highlanders' costume. We learn that they delighted in variegated and striped garments and that their favourite colours were purple and blue—ideal for concealment in the heather. However, the majority of them preferred dark brown, 'imitating nearly the leaves of the heather, that when lying upon the heath in the day, they may not be discovered by the appearance of their clothes. . . .'. How very unsuitable many of our modern 'clan' tartans would have been for this highly necessary purpose!

The similarity in dress between the Irish and the Scots up to the sixteenth century is obvious. However, in the year 1594 an event took place which provides us with one of the earliest hints of a costume which we can claim as truly Scottish. A party of Highlanders went over to Ireland to join the forces of Red Hugh O'Donnell in his fight against the

19

English. Their distinctive appearance is described by a contemporary writer:

> 'They are recognised among the Irish Soldiers by the distinction of their arms and clothing, their habits and language, for their exterior dress was mottled cloaks of many colours with a fringe to their shins and calves, their belts were over their loins outside their cloaks.'

Here we have the hint of a landmark in our story of Highland dress: the evolution of the belted plaid. Whereas in former times the various loose garments, mantles and cloaks could be worn in a variety of ways, the belted plaid had a discernible style of its own. A chaplain who visited Scotland in 1689 describes it as a multipurpose garment of definite proportions, worn in a specific style:

> 'They are constant in their habit or way of clothing; pladds are most in use with 'em, which . . . not only served them for cloaths by day in case of necessity but were pallats or beds in the night at such time as they travelled. . . . These pladds are about seven or eight yards long, differing in fineness according to the abilities or fancy of the wearers. They cover the whole body with 'em from the neck to the knees, excepting the right arm, which they mostly keep at liberty. Many of 'em have nothing under these garments besides wastcoats and shirts, which descent no lower than the knees, and they so gird 'em about the middle as to give 'em the same length as the linen under 'em, and thereby supply the defect of drawers and breeches.'

The rest of the dress consisted of sewn-up stockings of the same material as the plaid, tied below the knee with tufted garters. The shoes were without heels and had a very thin sole. The bonnets were blue, grey or 'sad colour'd as the purchaser thinks fit; and . . . sometimes lined according to the quality of their master'.

By the mid-sixteenth century we have some pictorial evidence of Highland costume. In 1562 a rather fanciful book entitled *Receuil de la diversité des Habits* was published in Paris. The two figures which are of particular interest to us consist of a Savage Scot and a Savage Captain, both of whom could serve to illustrate Irish or Scottish costume of the period (see over). The Captain wears a fringed cloak of what might be a herring-bone pattern but certainly could not be described as tartan. He also wears a highly imaginative helmet and a pair of fancy high boots. The quantity of arms he carries appears to be excessive for normal aggressive purposes and might represent a successful haul of loot. The Savage Scot is a female and seems to be wearing a winter costume consisting of a voluminous cloak of sheepskin.

Much more convincing is a water-colour painting in a book written and illustrated by Lucas de Heere, who lived as an exile in England from 1567 to 1577. This book may well have been designed as a guide for the use of his many fellow refugees from the Low Countries. It includes an excellent collection of illustrations of British costume.

The 'Schotsche Hooglander' is a tall impressive figure with long hair, armed with a dirk at his waist and a large claymore under his arm. He is dressed in a short tunic with long sleeves and a short pleated skirt. Over his shoulder he wears a large mantle, and on his feet flat shoes or brogues.

When the original manuscript was reproduced the drawings were unfortunately done in black and white. However, an examination of the original in the library of Ghent University reveals a most interesting fact. The mantle is of a pinkish shade, and the tunic is of a pale yellow with green diagonal stripes. The original colouring indicates quite clearly that he is wearing a tight pair of shorts of a bluish colour ending well above the knee.

Now here is an item of Scottish dress which has never been investigated in detail. Bishop Lesley, author of *De origine, moribus et rebus gestis Scotorum*, published in Rome in 1578, writes of *foemoralia simplicissima*, which we translate as 'a covering for the thighs of the simplest kind'. But he then

21

French version of 'Wild Scots', 1562

goes on to say that they were designed 'more for decency than for show or defence against cold'. Surely, then, this describes not the trews covering the whole leg, but short trews as depicted by Lucas de Heere. If we look closely at the eighth-century Book of Kells we will find a marginal drawing of a man in jacket and short trews. A carved cross at Monasterboice illustrates the same garment which is also described as Irish costume in a twelfth-century saga.

Evidence of the scanty clothing of the sixteenth-century Scots crops up in the most unexpected places. I have just come upon a contemporary engraving of 'Scoti nudi pugnantes' at the victory of the Spanish army at Gembloux in 1578.

As the saffron shirts and tunics of the Highlanders declined in use it became necessary to secure the plaid, particularly below the waist. This was done by means of a belt which gave its name to the new garment. The importance of the belted plaid in the history of costume lies partly in the fact that it was the progenitor of the stitched-up kilt which is worn today.

We have already mentioned the reference to what could be called a belted plaid in use by the Highlanders in Ireland in 1594. With the dawn of the seventeenth century comes a significant increase in the number and detail of such accounts.

John Taylor, who described himself as 'the King's Majesties Water-Poet', came to Scotland in 1618 and subsequently published an account of his 'Pennyless Pilgrimage', assuring his readers of its truth. Following a visit to the Braes of Mar, he gives one of the earliest accounts of Highland dress being worn for a special occasion by people who did not normally wear it.

Taylor states that for the month of August, and sometimes for part of September, many of the nobility and gentry of the kingdom came to the Highlands in order to hunt, and during their visit they conformed to the dress of the Highlanders:

'Their habite is shooes with but one sole apiece; stockings (which they call short hose) made of a warm stuffe of divers colours, which they call Tartane; as for breeches, many of them, nor their forefathers, never wore any, but a jerkin of the same stuffe that their hose is of, their garters being bands or wreathes of hay or straw, with a plead about their shoulders, which is a mantle of divers colours, much finer and lighter stuffe than their hose, with blue flat caps on their heads, a handkerchiefe knit with two knots about their necke; and thus they are attyred.'

An attempt has been made to interpret the 'jerkin of the same stuffe' as an early and unique reference to the little kilt in general use a century later. I cannot accept this and prefer to regard a jerkin as a jerkin.

Writing some twenty years later, James Gordon, the Parson of Rothiemay, describes the trews (which he says are for winter use) and the belted plaid. The trews are the long ones covering the entire legs and feet, over which they wear Rullions, or raw leather shoes. His description of the belted plaid is precise:

It is a 'loose Cloke of several Ells, striped and party colour'd, which they gird breadth-wise with a Leathern Belt so as it scarce covers the knees, and that for the above-mention'd Reason, that it may be no Lett to them, when on a Journey or doing any Work. Far the greatest part of the Plaid covers the uppermost parts of the Body. Sometimes it is all folded round the Body about the region of the Belt, for disengaging and leaving the Hands free; and sometimes 'tis wrapped round all that is above the Flank'.

We now know what the belted plaid looked like and how it was worn. It was simply a rectangular piece of cloth usually about 12 to 18 feet in length and about 5 feet in width. It is this simplicity which makes it unlike any other form of Highland dress worn before or after.

In order to put it on—we learn from a later writer—the

wearer had first to lay it out on the ground. The length of it was then reduced to about 4 or 5 feet by pleating the material over but leaving an unpleated panel about 2 feet wide at each end. The wearer then lay down on top of the plaid, on his back, with one edge of the pleats just above the back of his knees, the pleats being parallel with his spine. He then folded one of the unpleated panels across his stomach, and then the other on top. He was now wearing something like the modern kilt below his waist, and in order to keep it in place he merely girded a belt around his waist and stood up. However, although he had a fairly reasonably organised form of covering below the waist, he still had to do something with all the material which cascaded over his belt. There were several ways in which he could arrange this spare material according to his proposed activities or even the weather.

We are fortunate in having a number of eighteenth-century illustrations of some of the styles in which the belted plaid was worn. The best of these consists of a set of excellent engravings by a certain Van der Gucht who was working in London during the time that the Black Watch were there in 1743. Although the prints illustrate the military Highland dress, we are only concerned here with the main garment, the belted plaid, worn in the same way by soldier and civilian (see over).

The simplest arrangement shows the plaid hanging down over the belt at the back and reaching the calves. The front is open showing the kilted portion below the belt. The next plate shows this upper and outer portion drawn over the shoulders, and the artist explains that this is the way in which it is worn during rainy weather. The third plate shows 'A High-lander, that stands centry and walking with his cloke gathered up by half'. The upper portion of the belted plaid is hitched up by one corner on to the shoulder. This allows freedom of action to use the musket, sword and dirk. The little shoulder plaid worn with certain modern Highland dress is a relic of the style shown in this print.

About eighty years before the Van der Gucht engravings (see page 27), J. Michael Wright, a Scot, portrayed in oils

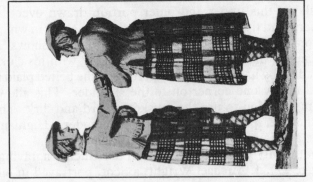

Engravings by Van der Gucht, showing the belted plaid, 1743

26

Highland Chief by J. Michael Wright, c. 1660

'Highland Chief'. Three versions of this picture are known, but the best can be seen in the Scottish National Portrait Gallery in Edinburgh. This life-size portrait shows an elegant figure wearing a belted plaid of several shades of brown and red with crimson and black stripes. Dr A. E. Haswell Miller, a former Keeper of the Gallery, and I, tried unsuccessfully to work out any evidence of a pattern or sett of this tartan.

The chief wears a slashed doublet over a full-sleeved shirt, a head-dress with a large white feather, tartan hose with castellated tops and large golden yellow garters, and flat shoes strapped above the ankle. He is armed with a long gun and powder horn, pistol, dirk and basket-hilted broadsword.

Michael Wright also painted a portrait of 'Lacy the Actor' in Highland dress, now in the Royal Collection. Our 'Highland Chief' is certainly in a theatrical pose.

Another picture in the Scottish National Portrait Gallery shows Kenneth, 3rd Lord Duffus, who died in 1734, wearing a belted plaid predominantly coloured in black, red, yellow and white stripes.

Richard Waitt painted some fine portraits of members of Clan Grant, including two of clansmen as opposed to chiefs or chieftains. The first, dated 1714, is of Alastair Grant Mor, known as 'The Champion', and is often wrongly claimed as a portrait of Rob Roy. He wears a belted plaid with a corner attached to his shoulder, as does a 'Piper to the Laird of Grant', depicted on a companion portrait. The tartan of the two men is similar and consists of golden yellow, red and grey stripes, with fine black lines. The yellow lines of the Piper's tartan have black edging, while the Champion's have white edging.

There are many more pictures of this period showing the belted plaid, and in 1723 the tartan jacket appears in a portrait of Major James Fraser of Castle Leathers (see opposite). The old cloth or velvet doublet had by then gone out of general use and the short tartan coat, or *còta-goirid*, replaced it, Major Fraser's jacket and trews are of the same tartan, but his plaid is of a different tartan.

28

Major Fraser of Castle Leathers, 1670-1750

The word *plaide* is Gaelic for blanket, and it was worn with the trews. It was quite a different piece of costume from the belted plaid (Gaelic, *fhéilidh-Mor* or *breacan an fhéilidh*).

The trews (Gaelic, *triubhas*), as worn by Major Fraser, are illustrated here for the first time in an oil-painting. The wearing of the trews had, of course, been well documented in contemporary accounts and engravings for centuries before this date.

There are many other fine pictures of the trews, and although it is not the purpose of this work to deal with military dress, reference must be made to Sir Henry Raeburn's portrait of Sir John Sinclair of Ulbster, painted in 1794 (see opposite). He is shown in the uniform of the Rothesay and Caithness Fencibles, which he raised that year. Sir John was Member of Parliament for Caithness, compiler of *The First Statistical Account of Scotland*, and a man who did not express his opinion without thought. He was convinced that the ancient form of Highland dress which should be preserved and worn was the trews. Accordingly he dressed his troops in tartan trousers and appears in his portrait similarly dressed. Whereas the old trews were like trunk hose with feet attached, the tartan trousers were of a more practical nature. He also wears a tartan plaid over the shoulder as another traditional reminder. Sir John emphasised his opinion by composing a rather gory marching song to be sung lustily by his men, who eventually mustered a thousand strong:

'Let others boast of philibeg,
    Of kilt and belted plaid,
Whilst we the ancient trews will wear,
    In which our fathers bled.'

The portrait paintings of Sir Henry Raeburn advanced the status of Highland costume. His style and techniques became widely acclaimed. Moreover, the romantic atmosphere of his paintings coincided with the romantic writings of his friend Sir Walter Scott. Robert Louis Stevenson said

30

Sir John Sinclair by Sir Henry Raeburn, 1794

that Raeburn's portraits, 'compared with the sort of living people one sees about the streets . . . are as bright as new sovereigns to fishy and obliterated sixpences'.

About 1798 Raeburn painted Sir Evan Murray MacGregor of MacGregor—at that time a teenager. He wears a tartan suit and stands in the same manner as Sir John Sinclair. His suit has long trousers.

Raeburn's portrait of Neil Gow, the famous Scottish fiddler, shows him wearing breeches over stockings, both of a simple broad-striped tartan. The fiddler in the picture of a Highland dance painted by David Allan, is identical. The dance took place on the Athol estate in the summer of 1780, and the main male character wears a pair of tartan trews gartered below the knee, and thus admirably suited to his lively leaping.

When proscription was repealed in 1782, the continuation of Highland dress relied on the uniform of the Highland regiments. We have seen that the belted plaid and the trews were in use up to the end of the eighteenth century, but so far there has been no reference to the 'little kilt' in the form in which it is worn today. In the history of costume rarely is there a precise date when it can be said that a particular costume came into use in a general manner. Styles might have been invented but their adoption usually evolved. There was nearly always a considerable overlap, and this was the case with the 'little kilt'.

The Kilt

THE kilt as we know it today almost certainly originated early in the eighteenth century. The word 'kilt' was not used by the Gaelic-speaking Highlander; he described it as the *Feileadh Beag*, which meant the 'little wrap', to distinguish it from the *Feileadh Mor*, the 'big wrap'. The former was often Anglicised as 'philabeg'.

It has already been pointed out that in order to make a kilt out of a belted plaid all one has to do is to cut the latter garment around the waist and remove the upper portion. Such an idea was obviously well within the inventive powers of the Highlander. Who then would suggest that the original idea had come to an Englishman, who in turn might be given the credit of having invented the kilt? In fact just such a suggestion was made over two hundred years ago by a Mr Baillie of Aberiachan, a man of good education and position and a member of a Highland family living beside Loch Ness.

Baillie wrote a letter dated 22nd March 1768, which was published in the *Edinburgh Magazine* for March 1785, and it might be that its contents surprised even the editor, who entitled the column 'The Felie-Beg, no part of the Ancient Highland Dress'. Anyway, at the time there was no storm of protest, nor indeed any reaction at all to Baillie's statement, which was based on his own personal knowledge and that of 'persons of credit', that the piece of Highland dress, 'termed in the Gaelic *felie-beg*, and in our Scots *little kilt*, is rather of late than ancient usage'. He went on to describe the Englishman's invention in detail:

'About fifty years ago, one Thomas Rawlinson, an Englishman, conducted an iron work carried on in the countries of Glengarie and Lochaber; he had a throng of Highlanders employed in the service, and became very fond of the Highland dress, and wore it in the neatest form; which I can aver as I became personally acquainted with him above 40 years ago. He was a man of genius and quick parts, and thought it no great stretch of invention to abridge the dress, and make it handy and convenient for his workmen; and accordingly directed the using of the lower part plaited of what is called the *felie* or *kilt* as above, and the upper part was set aside; and this piece of dress, so modelled as a diminutive of the former, was in the Gaelic termed *felie-beg* (*beg* in that tongue signifies *little*) and in our Scots termed *little kilt*. . . .'

Accordingly, the new garment was found so convenient that its use quickly spread in the Highlands and also in the 'Northern Low Countries'. Baillie said that until then (about 1725) he had never seen the little kilt used. Neither, in fact, had his father, a well-known Highlander born in 1655.

As one might expect, the letter came to be regarded sceptically by some of the Highland chiefs of the Revival Period in the 1820s. Stewart of Garth considered it to be an attack on the traditions of the Highlander; but Sir John Sinclair, a champion of all things Highland, wrote in 1830, '. . . it is well known that the phillibeg was invented by an Englishman in Lochaber about sixty years ago'.

General Stewart, the distinguished son of a Perthshire family, and author of *Sketches of the Character, Manners and Present State of the Highlanders*, published in 1822, the year of King George the Fourth's visit to Scotland, was one of the principal organisers of that highly romantic and flamboyant event. Up to that year he had spent most of his adult life serving in his regiment out of Scotland. Sir John Sinclair, on the other hand, born eighteen years earlier than Stewart, had a vast knowledge of Scottish life.

General Stewart's lack of evidence, and his statement that the people held 'a universal belief that the feile-beg had been part of their garb as far back as tradition reaches', was remarked upon in *The Costume of the Clans* (1845). The authors of this monumental volume, which weighs twenty-two pounds, describe themselves as John Sobieski Stolberg

Stuart and Charles Edward Stuart. I have been fortunate enough to examine many of their letters, paintings, poems and carvings in private collections, and to visit many of the places where they stayed.

The two brothers maintained that they were the sons of the legitimate son of Prince Charles Edward Stuart, the Young Pretender, by his wife Princess Louise Stolberg. They were received by some of Scotland's greatest families but denounced by others as imposters. I have described their claims and counter-claims and examined their publications in considerable detail in my *History of Highland Dress*.

In *Blackwood's Magazine* for April 1895, Miss Macdonell of Glengarry wrote that about 1837, when the brothers were in Edinburgh, they were talked of as 'the Princes'. She also credits them with the invention of the Dress Stuart tartan and the Hunting Stuart tartan. They had been heard talking about these tartans during their stay at Glengarry.

It was in fact the subject of tartans which did much to discredit them in the eyes of Sir Walter Scott and many Scottish antiquarians and scholars. In 1842 they published the handsome *Vestiarium Scoticum*, bound in red leather and bearing a variation of the King of Scots' armorial achievement in gilt. The authors claimed that it was based on 'a small black-leather quarto of the sixteenth century . . . once in the possession of the historian and faithful adherent of Queen Mary, John Lesley bishop of Ross'. It is probably the most controversial costume book ever written. For over a century both the book and its authors have been the subject of speculation and argument. In 1962 I wrote that the brothers were fully capable of forging the manuscript on which this book was said to be based. I gave as their possible motive an attempt to strengthen their claim to Royal descent by producing relics which might have been passed to them from Prince Charles Edward Stuart's personal possessions.

Whereas *The Costume of the Clans* is a most valuable work on the subject of Highland dress, the *Vestiarium Scoticum is* plainly a forgery. Nevertheless, it gives us an important list of tartans of the early 1840s, many of them appearing there for the first time. They are divided into two categories, 'Highland Clans' and 'The Lowland Houses and Border Clans'. Seventy-five colour plates illustrate the tartans.

Returning to the history of the kilt we must again refer to *The Costume of the Clans*, in which a picture of Alasdair Ruadh Macdonnell, who died in 1761, is said to show the first portrayal of the little kilt. If in fact the earliest illustration of the kilt is in this Glengarry picture—which, judging by the approximate age of Alasdair Ruadh, could have been painted about 1747, when he was released from The Tower—then such a fact could be very significant. Our perplexing English inventor worked in Glengarry, and if we are to believe John Sobieski Stuart, 'the new garment immediately attracted the notice of Ian MacAlasdair Mhic Raonnill of Glengarry'. The portrait is of none other than his son, and the Sobieski Stuart brothers, while staying with the Glengarry of their day, had from him the story of his ancestor and the invention of the kilt.

In this portrait of Young Glengarry he wears the belted plaid, and it is his henchman, standing slightly behind him, who wears the little kilt. John Sobieski Stuart describes it as 'the first specimen of this reduced member of the belted plaid with which we are acquainted, and which, like all others of the original form, is plaited throughout its entire circumference'. If we look at the portrait of Lord Duffus, painted about 1700 and now in the Scottish National Portrait Gallery, we will notice this arrangement of pleating all round the lower portion of his belted plaid. To the costume historian this forms a happy link with the kilt worn by Glengarry's henchman.

The David Morier picture of Culloden (described in the chapter on tartans) shows the little kilt in use at that battle. However, my favourite contemporary painting of the little kilt is the dual portrait of the Macdonald Boys, painted about 1750, when Highland dress was proscribed (see opposite). Sir James Macdonald, born in 1740, wears a tartan jacket, long tartan waistcoat and kilt, each of a different sett, none of which corresponds to the present-day Macdonald tartan.

36

The Macdonald Boys, c. 1750

Another delightful picture painted at that time emphasises why the neat little kilt gained rapid popularity. It depicts Sir Stuart Threipland of Fingask in a belted plaid so bulky that only with the greatest difficulty could he have passed through the average doorway. Sir Stuart was a fugitive after Culloden, and the picture shows him being advised by his guardian angel to take an alternative route lest he fall into the hands of the Government troops.

The kilt in caricature flourished in John Kay's *Edinburgh Portraits* (1837-38) in which the good folk of the capital are mercilessly portrayed with all their human failings. The prints bear dates and show men and women, many of them Highlanders with their ladies. We find the influence of the military style on civilian Highland dress in Kay's portrait of the Marquis of Graham and the Earl of Buchan. The merging of the two styles is again shown in Raeburn's magnificent portrait of The Macnab. This chief has been described as being of giant stature and strength, trying to ignore a load of inherited debts, and noted for his many eccentricities and tremendous pride of race. Although he was a major in the Breadalbane Volunteers, he is not wearing a correct military uniform in the portrait, but a mixture of military and civilian costume.

In the field of caricature, the prize must go to the French artists who worked in Paris during the occupation of that city by the Allied troops after the Battle of Waterloo. One of the favourites in my collection is '*Les Écossais à Paris, ou la curiosité des femmes*' (see opposite). It poses the age-old question as to what the Highlander wears under his kilt. The artist has been delicate enough to perpetuate the mystery.

It was not only the ladies of Paris who were intrigued by the secrets of Highland costume. None other than the Emperor of Russia demanded to know all. Having had a party of soldiers from the Highland regiments parade before him at the Palace Élysée, he lifted up the kilt of Sergeant Thomas Campbell 'so that he might not be deceived'.

Mention has already been made of the visit of King George the Fourth to Edinburgh in 1822. This Royal Occasion was

Les Écossais à Paris, ou la curiosité des femmes, *Paris, 1815*

commemorated in song and story, print and pottery, some serious but most with a sense of humour. Glengarry declared: 'They have no right to burlesque the national character and dress of real Highlanders.' But what is a 'real' Highlander? Lord Cockburn declared that 'The affectation of Celticism was absurd and rather nauseous. Hundreds who had never seen heather had the folly to array themselves in tartan'.

Absurd and nauseous it might be to some, but to others the sight of a Highlander, real or bogus, has aroused romantic sentiments hard to explain. *Blackwood's Edinburgh Magazine* of September 1822 responded with no uncertain patriotism:

'Then came marching along, to their wild native music, chieftains and clans—the descendants of those heroic and loyal warriors, who, true to their Prince, within less than a hundred years ago had pierced with their claymores into the very heart of England. They were now conducting their lawful—their hereditary Prince, down to Holyrood—and a fine spirit it was in that Prince that demanded their presence, and enjoyed the tossing of their plumes, their warlike and stormy music, and the varied splendour of the garb of Old Gaul.'

Equally aroused was George Muir, who described himself as 'a poor and Untutored Bard, but a true and loyal Scotsman'. After being present at the King's visit, he wrote:

'When, lo! a chieftain of our Isle arose,
Deck'd in the garb which oft dismayed our foes;
Upon his head was placed the bonnet blue,
Bedeck'd with massy plumes of sable hue;
In tartan was the graceful youth arrayed,
Across his manly shoulders hung the plaid,
A brace of pistols belted to his side,
With dirk and broad claymore—our nation's pride.

On different places on his garment hung,
Scotia's dear emblem, by the bards oft sung,
Surrounded with the hardy-blooming heath,
That presses on the foe, when armed with death.'

The most splendid picture of the King in Highland dress is the portrait by Sir David Wilkie in the collection of Her Majesty the Queen. Larger than life, it shows him wearing a red tartan jacket, shoulder plaid and kilt. His pistols, dirk and broadsword are carefully painted, and his elegant posture and noble figure contrast with the caricatures.

In St Leonard's Street, Edinburgh, stood a rubble-built tenement of three storeys and an attic, known as the 'Castle of Clouts'. Its proprietor was a wealthy tailor called Hunter whose first shop was in the Lawnmarket. The family business was described as 'Army Contractors and Clothiers', but their claim to fame was the fact that they supplied the King with his Highland tartans and accoutrements.

The most expensive of these, costing £375, was a fine gold-chased head ornament for his bonnet, consisting of the Royal Scots Crown in miniature, set with diamonds, pearls, rubies and emeralds, supported on a wreath of chased gold thistles surrounding a large sea-green emerald.

The next most expensive item was the King's Highland dirk, the knife and dirk blades being inlaid with gold, the small fork being made of silver, and the top of the dirk being crowned with a sea-green emerald. The crimson-velvet scabbard was ornamented with chased gold mountings with the Royal Arms of St Andrew, the Thistle, etc.

The basket-hilted broadsword had a hilt of polished steel inlaid with gold, and the blade was inlaid likewise. The other weapons consisted of a pair of polished steel Highland pistols, inlaid all over.

Other items included a fine white goatskin sporran with massive gold purse-top chased with the Royal Arms, and ornamented with nine rich gold-bullion tassels, a powder-horn richly mounted with fine gold and Scottish gems, belts and a pair of fine gold-filigree shoe rosettes studded with gems.

The tartans consisted of 61 yards of 'Royal Sattin Plaid' at seventeen shillings a yard, 31 yards of 'Royal Plaid Velvet' at thirty-six shillings a yard, and 17½ yards 'Royal Plaid Casemere' at thirty-six shillings a yard.

By this time the firm of George Hunter and Company had opened a shop at 25 Princes Street, to which a constant throng of people went to see the King's magnificent accoutrements.

The King wore this Highland costume at the Levee which was held at Holyrood Palace on 17th August and attended by a vast concourse of the Scottish nobility. As he dressed at Dalkeith Palace where he was staying, he is said to have remarked, "I cannot help smiling at myself".

Sir David Wilkie made some delightful drawings of the Drawing Room which was held three days after the Levee and which was attended by some three hundred ladies of rank. Wilkie wrote to his sister that it contained 'a very unfair sample of our Scottish ladies', and that on being presented the King kissed them upon the cheek 'gracefully, respectfully and gently, and looking as grave as possible all the time. It was what it ought to be, a mere ceremony'.

The scurrilous caricaturists thought otherwise, and one anonymous engraving shows the King in a very brief kilt embracing a singularly unattractive lady—in fact on the occasion of the Drawing Room he wore a Field Marshal's uniform. The print is entitled 'A Thousand Warm Receptions in the North', and it also shows Sir William Curtis, a former Lord Mayor of London, in Highland dress.

Sir William and the King are again shown in burlesque Highland dress in another anonymous engraving entitled 'Equipt for a Northern Visit' (see opposite). In this print the King reprimands Curtis for appearing such a freak, and indeed he was a figure of fun and no compliment to His Majesty in Highland dress. George Cruickshank published an engraving of Curtis wearing a ridiculous bonnet, and tartan jacket and kilt ill-suited to his vast girth. Scott's

King George IV and Sir William Curtis, 1822

son-in-law, Lockhart, wrote that 'This portentous appari-
tion cast an air of ridicule and caricature over the whole of Sir
Walter's celtified pageantry'.

Perhaps the most elegant portrait of a chief dressed for the
Royal Occasion is that of Sir Evan Macgregor of Macgregor,
painted by George Watson. The highly elaborate costume is
worn with style despite the enormous size of the sporran, the
broadsword, large dirk, pistols worn over the bulky plaid,
tartan jacket and kilt.

There are indeed many fine portraits of the 1822 costumes, including Macdonnell of Glengarry by Sir Henry
Raeburn, to be seen in the National Gallery of Scotland.
There are also many examples of the actual clothing and
accoutrements still extant.

Illustrations of kilted Victorians are legion and might be
classified as the Pompous Period. However, many of them
have considerable dignity, largely due to the influence of Sir
Edwin Landseer and his portraits of the Royal Family. Following the visit of Queen Victoria and Prince Albert to
Scotland in 1842, and the Prince's subsequent adoption of
Highland dress, it became an almost essential costume for
sport and evening-wear by the many followers of the Court
styles.

The dress known as 'Highland' and worn throughout
Scotland—largely by the new lairds, sporting-tenants and
their servants—was now vastly different from the clothes
worn in the Highlands over a century earlier. The romantic
concept flourished and was popularised by McIan, an artist
who painted Victorians disguised as eighteenth-century
Highlanders, and whose work can be seen today in most
establishments in Scotland boasting a 'Highland' atmosphere.

At the age of thirty-six, Robert McIan abandoned the
south-west of England and the London stage to become what
he described as 'The Veritable Highlandman'. In col-
laboration with James Logan he produced his two-volume
collection of colour-plates entitled *Clans of the Scottish Highlands*. Logan's descriptions of the 'hospitable tribes' met

with instant approval by Victorian gentility, and their next publication, *Gaelic Gatherings* (1848), depicted the Highlanders 'in their pastoral, agricultural, piscatorial, and hunting occupations'. Despite their inaccuracies and distortions, the McIan prints still sell today as prints, table-mats, postcards, etc. They show the Highlander as a symbol of adventurous and romantic life.

Prince Charles Edward Stuart

BEFORE returning to the main theme of Highland dress, let us look at the costume of the Prince about whose clothing so much fantasy has been created and perpetuated. Only a brave modern artist would portray him in anything other than a full Highland costume. Indeed, it is considered to be almost essential that he appear on stage or screen fully tartaned and looking 'Bonnie'. Surely such an adventurous and fascinating character deserves a better fate at the hand of history.

One of the best-known and least likely pictures is 'Bonnie Prince Charlie', by John Pettie. For over half a century it has promoted the sale of Highland whisky and liqueur, biscuits and toffees. Pettie was a highly romantic Victorian, born in 1839, and his subjects range from the dramatic 'Sword-and-Dagger Fight' to the sentimental 'Two Strings to Her Bow'. He was greatly inspired by the novels of Sir Walter Scott, and his concept of the 'Bonnie Prince', shared by many of his contemporaries, has lived on.

These imaginary 'Portraits' of the Prince are far removed from the much more interesting portraits painted during his lifetime which replace the image of a romantic mannequin with a human being portrayed within the artistic conventions of his time. But it is his costume which concerns us, and for any Highland elements we must examine the middle period of his life, between the elegant days in Italy and the unhappy period of his old age.

These middle-period portraits were intended to serve as political propaganda and obviously show him in the best possible light. It is surprising, therefore, that Highland dress, when he wears it, is not shown in a more convincing way. There is, of course, no evidence of him ever having been painted in Highland dress in Scotland. Indeed, the first portrait with a Scottish bias is an adaptation of an earlier court portrait. The original painting was by Antoine David, a popular portrait painter in Rome. This portrait was subsequently engraved by Edelinck, who then produced a second version of the Prince wearing court dress but this time with a circular Highland bonnet perched on his head. He also wears a white cockade, and although the engraving was produced about 1740, the portrait was painted about ten years before.

Many small portraits based on the David painting were sent over to Scotland for propaganda purposes during the period of the Jacobite Rising. The alterations to give a Scottish flavour varied. The portraits were reproduced in the form of miniatures, small engravings, and on the lids of snuff boxes. They were also engraved on drinking-glasses—which are most desirable collectors' pieces today. It has been pointed out that the Prince himself must have found these items fascinating, for he had never visited Scotland.

Of a similar nature are the numerous propaganda portraits based on the Blanchet painting of the Prince showing signs of maturity. There are many versions and many forms of this portrait, and the majority of the miniature reproductions show him wearing elements of Highland dress.

Sir Robert Strange was a young artist in Edinburgh who painted the Prince when he visited the city. His portrait is perhaps less flattering than others, but it may be that it was the only one done from life during the Prince's visit to Scotland. Strange was one of the Prince's great admirers and acted as a bodyguard during the Jacobite campaign of 1745. He engraved the portrait, and a great number of miniatures were based on it. The most interesting miniature is one which is said to have been presented to 'the Gentle Lochiel' by the Prince. Possibly the earliest known portrait of the Prince showing a complete Highland dress, it depicts him wearing a tartan coat and a flat bonnet with a white cockade. The tartan is most carefully painted and consists of red and black stripes with a white line. Another version of this miniature in the Scottish National Portrait Gallery has a piece of tartan attached to it, reputed to have been worn by the

Prince, but the sett is different and the colours consist of dark blue and red stripes with thin black and white lines.

Perhaps the most extraordinary series of portraits is that known as the 'Harlequin' type. Charles is shown wearing a tartan jacket and breeches, and white gaiters coming up to the knee. He has a little round bonnet, with white cockade, perched flat on top of his head, and what might be described as a pantomime sword. This portrait appears on many glass engravings and snuff boxes, and was obviously very popular. In some versions he wears large gauntlets.

Many pictures have been wrongly described as portraits of the Prince, and one such is a beautiful painting in oils by Hans Hysing (see opposite). It was known and exhibited as 'Prince Charles Edward Stuart' for many years, despite the fact that it was signed and dated 1726, at which time the Prince was six years old. This fine portrayal of the trews, tartan jacket and plaid was engraved and published as a portrait of the Prince in at least three publications. The subject is in fact the Duke of Leeds.

The caricatures of the Prince in Highland dress cannot be taken as serious evidence; however, they give an indication of certain attitudes towards the Highland costume. One of the caricatures is interesting because it was engraved in 1745 by Richard Cooper, who was a teacher of Sir Robert Strange (see page 50). It is entitled 'A likeness notwithstanding the Disguise that any Person who Secures the Son of the Pretender is Intitled to a Reward of £30,000'. The Prince wears a large bonnet, a tartan jacket and plaid, and tartan breeches coming to just below the knee, leaving a bare gap between them and his calf-length tartan hose. One thing which it does illustrate is the state of near chaos which the plaid can achieve.

The number of items of Highland dress and pieces of tartan said to have been worn by Prince Charles are legion. One item which must be taken seriously is the fragment of tartan attached to a volume of the original collection entitled *The Lyon in Mourning*, and now preserved in the National Library of Scotland. This very important collection of let-

The Duke of Leeds. Engraving after painting by Hans Hysing, 1726

Prince Charles Edward Stuart.
Engraving by Richard Cooper, 1745

ters, etc., was made by Bishop Forbes, who was arrested on his way to join the Prince in 1745. Below the fragment of tartan, Forbes wrote:

'The above are pieces of the outside and inside of that identical waistcoat which Macdonald of Kingsburgh gave to the Prince when he laid aside the woman's clothes. The said waistcoat being too fine for a servant the Prince exchanged it with Malcolm Macleod. Malcolm, after parting with the Prince, and finding himself in danger of being seized, did hide the waistcoat in a cleft of rock, where, upon his returning home in the beginning of September 1747, he found it all rotten to bits, except only as much as would serve to cover little more than one's loof [palm of the hand], and two buttons, all of which he was pleased to send to me. The waistcoat had lain more than a full year in the cleft of the rock, for Malcom Macleod was made prisoner sometime in July 1746.'

Apart from the value of the specimen of cloth, the above note indicates how at that time Highland clothing could be used as a means of identification. It also confirms the account of the Prince's wanderings after Culloden disguised as a woman, and how, after removing that disguise, he put on Highland clothes. Indeed, when he arrived soaking wet at an inn he is described as wearing 'a plaid without breeches, trews, or even philibeg'.

The Lyon in Mourning contains a number of references to Highland dress, including the statement that at the Battle of Culloden the Prince wore a tartan jacket and buff vest. There is also a graphic description of him at a later stage of his escape, when he was 'bare-footed, had an old black kilt coat on, a plaid, philabeg and waistcoat, a dirty shirt and a long red beard, a gun in his hand, a pistol and durk by his side'. How much more moving this authentic description is than the fancy images of 'Bonnie Prince Charlie', a title which Queen Victoria would not allow in her presence. It had to be 'Prince Charles Edward Stuart', and rightly so.

In the Lockhart Papers, published in 1817, we learn of the

Prince's interest in Highland dress. When a Highland officer met him aboard ship just before he landed, the Prince asked him if he was not cold in such a costume. The Highlander explained that it was his habitual dress and that he wrapped himself up in it at night. The Prince then asked how, if he was wrapped up in his plaid, he could leap up in the event of a sudden attack. To this he received the answer that in times of danger 'we had a different method of useing the plaid, that with one spring I could start to my feet with drawn sword and cock'd pistol in my hand without being in the least incomber'd with my bed-cloaths'.

Nearly every Scottish museum has at least one relic of the Prince's costume, but one of the most fascinating consists of a tartan coat and trews. These can be seen in the Scottish United Services Museum, Edinburgh Castle. Said to have been worn by him at Culloden, they were acquired by the Judge Advocate in Scotland from a lady who affirmed that the Prince had somehow left them in her house. Careful examination shows that the suit could only have been worn by a very thin youth under five feet in height with a 30-inch waist, a 30-inch chest and a shoulder width of approximately one foot.

The coat is of hard tartan of green, black, red, blue, white, yellow and violet. The warp and the weft differ slightly, and from a distance the tartan appears to be striped rather than checked. This difference in warp and weft is not uncommon in early tartans belonging to the pre-clan tartan period. The rather badly made trews consist of a number of pieces of tartan sewn together. The pattern is a simple green and red check forming approximately half-inch squares. These trews certainly do not match in size the pair in the West Highland Museum at Fort William, also said to have been worn by the Prince.

The number of relics said to have belonged to the Prince increases merrily every year. Contemporary accounts of him wearing 'Highland dress' usually meant that he had on a short tartan coat. Nevertheless, there is an early 'portrait' of him in a kilt and seated on a prancing charger, and another of him wearing what would be described today as tartan 'briefs'.

It is surprising that the caricaturists of the Prince did not make more of the disguise of a woman which he wore after Culloden. An attorney of Macclesfield, who saw him with his Highland army in 1745, described him as a 'very handsome person of a man rather tall, exactly proportioned and walks well'. Disguised as a woman, he was described as an 'odd muckle, illshapen wife'. Unfortunately we have no detailed account of his costume when he disguised himself as an Irish girl, 'an excellent spinstress', in the company of Flora Macdonald during his flight to Skye. There are a few portraits of him in disguise, but most of them are unconvincing.

There were of course many bogus portraits of the Prince. One character who was used as a stand-in for the Prince's so-called portrait was a handsome young Dane, Tycho Hofmann. A painting of him was engraved in 1745, and later became reincarnated as 'Prince Charles'. It then appeared on a print which also depicted him flanked by Flora Macdonald and Jenny Cameron, a fifty-year-old widow, dubbed by the Prince's opponents as his mistress. Both ladies are made 'Highland' by the addition of cross-hatching on their sleeves to suggest tartan. The whole question of women's costume as worn in the Highlands during those early periods has never been closely examined.

Highland Ladies

'Ye Caledonian beauties, who have long
Been both the muse and subject of my song,
Assist your bard, who, in harmonious lays,
Designs the glory of your Plaid to raise.'

So wrote Allan Ramsay, the Scottish wig-maker poet in 1720. However, the plaid of which he wrote was the silken symbol worn by ladies of fashion during the years following the Union. The styles of Edinburgh had little relationship to the costume of the women living in dire poverty in the remote Highlands who had to make do with what they could afford. Despite the fact that we cannot associate fashion with the clothing of the Highland peasant women, there were obviously degrees of style dependent on economics.

In 1688, William Sacheverell visited the island of Mull and later wrote an *Account* in which he states that 'the usual outward habit of both sexes is the pladd; the women's much finer; the colours more lively, and the squares larger than the men's and put me in mind of the ancient Picts. This serves them for a veil and covers both head and body'. It is interesting to compare this shape of covering with that illustrated in 1562, in the *Receuil*.

The General Assembly of the sixteenth century stipulated that 'all using of plaids in the Kirk by readers or ministers' was to stop, and their wives were 'to be subject to the same'. Indeed it was a time when careful thought was required in choosing ones clothes. A lady's profession might be suspected should she dress in a style above her station. An Act of 1567 warned that 'it be lawchfull to na women to weir abone hir estait except howres'.

In 1578 the Bishop of Ross published an account of women's costume in the Highlands, but obviously the ladies to whom he refers were not those of the poorer classes.

'Bot the cleithing fo the women with thame was maist decent. For thair cotes war syd evin to the hanckleth, wyd mantilis abone, or playdes all embroudiret artificiouslie, braclets about their armes, jewalis about thair neck, broches hinging at thair halse, baith cumlie and decent, and mekle to thair decore and outsett.'

Twenty years later a contrast was made by Fynes Moryson who wrote that the 'inferior sort of Citizen wives, and the women of the Countrey, did weare cloaks made of a course stuffe, of two or three colours in Checker worke, vulgarly called "Plodan" '.

Nowadays one hears reference to the Arisaid, particularly in country dancing. Its ancestor was a simple cloak fastened around the waist by a belt, and at the breast by a brooch, and descending to the heels. It would appear to have been made of plain or striped material.

The description given by another traveller, Martin Martin, at the end of the seventeenth century, refers to a woman of means, and because of its detail it is of considerable importance.

'The ancient Dress worn by the Women, and which is yet wore by some of the Vulger, called *Arisad*, is a white *Plade*, having a few small stripes of black, blew and red; it reached from the Neck to the Heels, and was tied before on the Breast with a Buckle of Silver or Brass, according to the Quality of the Person. I have seen some of the former of an hundred Marks value; it was broad as any ordinary Pewter Plate, the whole curiously engraved with various Animals etc. There was a lesser Buckle, which was wore in the middle of the larger, and above two Ounces weight; it had in the Center a large piece of Chrystal, or some finer Stone, and this was set all round with several finer Stones of a lesser size.

'The *Plad* being pleated all round, was tied with a Belt below the Breast; the Belt was of Leather, and several pieces of Silver intermixed with the Leather like a Chain.

The lower end of the Belt has a piece of Plate, about 8 inches long, and three in breadth, curiously engraven; the end of which was adorned with fine Stones or pieces of red Corral. They wore Sleeves of Scarlet Cloth, closed at the end as Mens Vests, with gold lace round 'em, having Plate Buttons set with fine stones. The Head dress was a fine *Kerchief* of Linen strait [i.e. tight] about the Head, hanging down the back taper-wise; a large Lock of Hair hangs down their Cheeks above their Breast, the lower end tied with a knot of Ribbands.'

There is considerable emphasis on jewellery, and in particular on brooches, in this fascinating account. These were the most important adornments of a Highland woman and many of them became family heirlooms which we can still admire today. The early masterpieces of the Scoto-Irish craftsmen illustrate the art-styles of the period and are often decorated in gold, silver or enamel. The later Highland brooches to which Martin Martin refers are circular in shape, often of brass bars hammered out flat. The surface is usually engraved and the animals, to which he also refers, are usually grotesque deer, hounds, birds, wild-cats, etc. Heart-shaped brooches were popular as love tokens and were also worn as protection against the evil eye.

During the early eighteenth century the quality and vitality of the craftsmanship declined and in some cases came under Lowland influence. The complex and stylish Celtic interlaced patterns lost their true spirit. However, even the later examples were vastly preferable to the circular silver plates with an ostentatious 'Cairngorm' in the centre which we see worn today, and which have the appearance of fried eggs.

Returning to earlier centuries we find some intriguing references to women's costume in Kirk Session Records. In Aberdeen, for instance, in the late sixteenth century, the wearing of plaids by women was forbidden, but in Elgin in 1602, Issobell Nauchtie being 'accusit of being fra the kirk pretendit the laik of a plaid'. In 1604, a Glasgow Kirk Session 'considering that great disorder hath been in the Kirk by women sitting with their heads covered with plaids during sermon sleeping, therefore ordains intimation to be made that afterward none sit with their head covered with plaids during sermon time'.

The ladies of Elgin appear to have been a particularly troublesome lot. According to the Kirk Session Records of March 1624, 'My Lord Byschop publictly from the pulpeit inhibetit the women to hald and wear the plaids about their heidss uncumly in the kirk the tyme of sermone, siclyk that they sitt nocht with ther bakkis to the pulpeit.' An Elgin lady of easy virtue could not seek anonymity when she faced the consequences of being found out. The Kirk Session ordained 'that fra this forth no woman fornicatrix be suffered to go to har publict repentance with a plaid about hir'.

In early seventeenth-century Edinburgh the plaid was frequently taken as the sign of a loose woman. Despite 'divers and sundrie laudibill actes and statutes' made by the Provost and Baillies, 'discharging that barbarous and uncivil habitte of women's wearing of plaids, yit such hes bein the impudencie of many of thame that they have continewit the foresaid babbarous habitte'.

Edward Burt's *Letters* (1754) describe the plaid as 'the undress of the ladies at Inverness and to a genteel woman who adjusts it with a good air, is a becoming veil'. He adds, however, that the garment to which he refers is made of silk or fine worsted, two breadths wide, and three yards in length. It is obviously an accessory and not a costume. Burt illustrates his *Letters* with drawings of Highlanders, one of whom is a woman, but as it is badly drawn we can only describe her costume as a long-sleeved garment, reaching to her ankles and fastened around her waist with a belt.

Among the portraits of the Grant family and their retainers, painted by Richard Waitt, is one entitled 'The Hen Wife', dated 1706. Unfortunately it is not a full-length portrait and only shows an elderly woman with a mantle over her head, but wearing a circular Highland brooch. There are, in fact, hardly any pictures of women in Highland costume during the eighteenth and early nineteenth centuries, other than those of lairds' ladies. Helen Balfour was painted by William Mosman in 1742, but although it is a full-length portrait, the only 'Highland' element is a tartan plaid hanging loosely around her shoulders.

One of the earliest and most delightful portraits of a Highland lady is that of Helen Murray of Ochtertyre, painted by an unknown artist but certainly belonging to the period of the Forty-Five (see opposite). She wears a dress of red tartan with dark blue, green or black stripes or lines. Furthermore, in order to make it quite clear where her sympathies lay, she holds in her extended left hand the White Rose of the Jacobite cause.

The renowned Flora Macdonald was painted by Allan Ramsay and Richard Wilson during her lifetime. Allan Ramsay painted her more than once, but the best-known picture shows her with a white rose in her hair, two white roses on her bosom, and a tartan plaid draped over her left shoulder and fastened to her right. Richard Wilson's portrait is slightly less flattering and shows her in a tartan dress with slashed sleeves, fastened down the front with three white cockades.

Jane, Duchess of Gordon, is said to have introduced tartan into Court fashion in 1792, and acquired the title of 'The Tartan Belle'. Certainly by the year 1812 tartan was high fashion in London and Paris, and the presence of Highland troops in Paris after the Battle of Waterloo continued to influence its vogue.

Queen Victoria's love of tartan is well known and she wore a long silk tartan scarf almost every evening while staying at Balmoral. The Royal children wore Highland dress in which they posed for Landseer and Winterhalter. Indeed, one of the Queen's Christmas presents to her Prince Consort was a painting by Sir Edwin Landseer in which she is shown wearing a skirt of a tartan-like pattern. These Victorian costumes were not 'Highland' dress, but merely the fashionable styles of the moment made of tartan material.

The idea of Victorian ladies in the kilt is quite unthinkable, but it had happened at the beginning of their evening. The following obituary notice appeared in the Inverness Journal of 17th July 1617:

Helen Murray of Ochtertyre, c. 1745

able, but it had happened at the beginning of their century. The following obituary notice appeared in the *Inverness Journal* of 17th July 1812:

'Died, lately in the parish of Knockando, County of Elgin, an eccentric character known as Red Jean, or Jean Roy. She disliked her own sex, and always pretended to be a man, wearing a kilt, jacket, and blue bonnet. She generally worked as a day labourer.'

Reading List

FOR the early periods *Old Irish and Highland Dress* by H. F. McClintock and John Telfer Dunbar (Dundalgen Press, 1949) is the only book covering that subject. *The History of Highland Dress* by John Telfer Dunbar (Oliver and Boyd, 1962) is the most comprehensive work covering the history of the costume, both civil and military, and it includes an appendix on early Scottish dyes.

The Costume of the Clans by John Sobieski Stolberg Stuart and Charles Edward Stuart (Edinburgh, 1845) contains a wealth of information requiring careful assessment. Their *Vestiarium Scoticum* (Edinburgh 1842) is a fascinating forgery.

There are many publications containing colour plates of tartan but, with a few exceptions, they avoid any account of them in the letterpress. An exception is *The Setts of the Scottish Tartans* by D. C. Stewart (Shepheard-Walwyn, 1974), the first book to define the patterns and investigate their origins.

The Official Tartan Map by John Telfer Dunbar and Don Pottinger (Elm Tree Books, 1976), published with the full authoritative approval of Clan Chiefs, the Standing Council of Scottish Chiefs and the Lord Lyon King of Arms, defines 140 tartans and gives information on tartan usage.

The most beautiful book on tartans is *Old and Rare Scottish Tartans* by D. W. Stewart, published in 1893, containing forty-five silk reproductions. The first book to contain a list of tartan setts is *The Scottish Gael* by James Logan, published in 1831.

Three important articles by pioneer writers on clan tartans are 'The Great Clan Tartan Myth' by Colonel M. M. Haldane (*Scotland's Magazine*, 1931), 'Tartan and Clan Tartans' by Major I. H. Mackay Scobie (*Chambers's Journal*, June 1942), and 'The Truth About the Tartan' by Dr A. E.

Haswell Miller (*Scotland's Magazine*, November 1947).

The following articles have been written by John Telfer Dunbar: 'The Bannockburn Tartans' (*Scotland's Magazine*, October 1963), 'The Veritable Highlandman' (R. R. McIan) (*Scotland's Magazine*, December 1956), 'Highlanders in Paris' (1815) (*Scotland's Magazine*, April 1950), 'Sir John Sinclair of Ulbster' (*Scotland's Magazine*, March 1956).